APP 1 4 2014

D0502942

EXTRAORDINARY WOMEN

Sonia
SOTOMAYOR

Brigid Gallagher

Chicago, Illinois

Edited by Abby Colich
Designed by Philippa Jenkins
Picture research by Ruth Blair
Production by Helen McCreath
Originated by Capstone Global Library
Printed and bound in China by Leo Paper
Group

17 16 15 14 13
10 9 8 7 6 5 4 3 2 1

Library of Congress Cataloging-in-
Publication Data
Gallagher, Brigid.
  Sonia Sotomayor / Brigid Gallagher.
  pages cm.—(Extraordinary women)
  Includes bibliographical references and
index.
  ISBN 978-1-4109-5946-1 (hb)—ISBN
978-1-4109-5954-6 (pb) 1. Sotomayor,
Sonia, 1954—Juvenile literature. 2. United
States. Supreme Court—Biography—Ju-
venile literature. 3. Hispanic American
judges—Biography—Juvenile literature. I.
Title.
  KF8745.S67G35 2014
  347.73'2634092—dc23
  2013017183   [B]

Acknowledgments

The author and publisher are grateful to
the following for permission to reproduce
copyright material: Alamy: p. 8 (© ZUMA
Press, Inc.); Corbis: pp. 4 (© JIM YOUNG/
Reuters), 7 (© Ron Sachs/CNP), 10 (©
White House/Handout/CNP), 14 (© White
House/Handout/CNP), 15 (© ARISTIDE
ECONOMOPOULOS/Star Ledger), 37
(© Wally McNamee), 38 (© Dennis Van
Tine./Retna Ltd), 41 (© White House/
Handout/CNP); Eyevine: pp. 12 (Polaris),
20 (Marilynn K. Yee/The New York Times),
24 (Marilynn K. Yee/The New York Times);
Getty Images: pp. 6 (The White House/
Handout), 7 (NY Daily News), 8 (CBS
Photo Archive), 9 (The White House/
Handout), 10 (The White House/Handout),
11 (J. SCOTT APPLEWHITE/AFP), 13
(Barry Winiker), 16 (Alex Wong), 18 (Bill
Pierce//Time Life Pictures), 19 (Michael
Kelley), 21 (Riccardo S. Savi/WireImage),
22 (Tom Williams/Roll Call), 23 (Tom
Williams/Roll Call), 25 (Terry Ashe/
Time & Life Pictures), 28 (Rick Maiman/
Bloomberg), 29 (BOB STRONG/AFP),
31 (Diana Walker/Time Life Pictures), 32
(Courtesy Court of Appeals/MCT), 34
(Bill Clark/Roll Call), 35 (Joshua Roberts/
Bloomberg), 36 (NY Daily News Archive),
40 (Jared Wickerham), 42 (Carolyn Kaster/
AFP), 43 (Alex Wong); PA Photos: pp. 30
(Mark Lennihan/AP), 33 (Adam Nadel/
AP); Rex Features: p. 39; Shutterstock: pp. 5
(© Brandon Bourdages), 35 (© K2 images);
Superstock: p. 17 (age fotostock).

Cover photograph of Sonia Sotomayor
reproduced with permission from Getty
Images (Mark Wilson).

Every effort has been made to contact
copyright holders of any material
reproduced in this book. Any omissions will
be rectified in subsequent printings if notice
is given to the publisher.

All the Internet addresses (URLs) given in
this book were valid at the time of going
to press. However, due to the dynamic
nature of the Internet, some addresses may
have changed, or sites may have changed
or ceased to exist since publication. While
the author and publisher regret any
inconvenience this may cause readers, no
responsibility for any such changes can
be accepted by either the author or the
publisher.

CONTENTS

Changing the Course of History

Sonia placed her left hand on the Bible that her mother, Celina, was holding. Her brother, Juan Jr., stood by her side. Sonia raised her right hand. Supreme Court Chief Justice John Roberts swore, or confirmed, her into office as associate justice of the United States Supreme Court (the highest court of law).

In front of hundreds of cameras that captured the moment for the nation, Sonia pledged to support and defend the Constitution of the United States. She promised to uphold justice for every American. "Congratulations and welcome to the court," Justice Roberts said as they shook hands.

Chief Justice John Roberts swore Sonia in as a justice of the Supreme Court.

The Supreme Court building is located in Washington, D.C., and was built in 1935.

First Hispanic Supreme Court Justice

Sonia, a woman from the Bronx who had grown up dreaming that one day she'd be a judge like the ones on the *Perry Mason* TV show, had achieved more than she'd ever hoped. She was officially a Supreme Court justice, which is the highest job possible in the legal profession. By exceeding her own goals, Sonia also changed the course of American history. She became the first Hispanic justice of the Supreme Court and only the third female justice in history.

BREAKING BOUNDARIES

THE AMERICAN DREAM

Sonia's story of success is an example of the American Dream. The American Dream is the idea that any United States citizen can succeed through hard work, courage, and determination. Sonia's hard work and willpower took her from the small Bronx apartment of her childhood to the Supreme Court building.

Sonia from the Bronx

Sonia's parents, Celina Báez Sotomayor and Juan Sotomayor, grew up in Puerto Rico, an island in the Caribbean. They met after Celina's service in the Women's Army Corps (WAC) during World War II. The couple fell in love and got married. After World War II, they eventually moved to a tenement in the Bronx, a borough (neighborhood) of New York City.

On June 25, 1954, Celina gave birth to their first child, Sonia Maria Sotomayor. Sonia was the first person in her family born in the United States. In 1957 the Sotomayors moved to the Bronxdale Houses, another apartment building in the Bronx. The same year, Sonia's little brother, Juan Jr., was born. He was nicknamed "Junior."

Baby Sonia poses for a photo with her parents, Juan Sr. and Celina.

6

People of all different cultures and backgrounds lived in the Bronxdale Houses.

New York Roots

Sonia likes to be called "Sonia from the Bronx" because she is proud of her New York roots. She watched New York Yankees games next to her father on the sofa, where he taught her the rules of baseball. She also read comics, such as *Archie* and *Richie Rich*. They helped her learn English, since Spanish was spoken at home.

Growing Up Nuyorican

Sonia has expressed great pride that she is both a New Yorker and of Puerto Rican descent. She is a Nuyorican, which is a combination of the terms "New Yorker" and "Puerto Rican." Many of her favorite childhood activities involved Hispanic traditions. At family parties, they listened to Latin American dance music and ate traditional Puerto Rican dishes.

Sonia remains close with her family, including her stepfather and mother, and sister-in-law and brother.

Childhood Challenges

Sonia loved to read—especially *Nancy Drew* books. In them the main character, Nancy, is a girl detective. Sonia wanted to be like Nancy Drew, so she decided that she was going to be a detective when she grew up. But when Sonia was seven, she was diagnosed with type 1 diabetes. Sonia's doctors told her that a career as a detective wasn't realistic.

Sonia dreamed of becoming a detective just like Nancy Drew.

Sonia began to learn about the United States court system by watching episodes of *Perry Mason*.

This did not discourage Sonia for long. She quickly realized, after watching episodes of the TV show *Perry Mason*, that she could do "some of the same things by being a lawyer." Watching *Perry Mason* helped Sonia understand what lawyers and judges did. After one episode, she realized that "the most important person" in the courtroom "was the judge.... I want to be that person," she decided.

TYPE I DIABETES

Diabetics such as Sonia must give themselves shots of insulin daily. Diabetes changed Sonia's life. She had to learn how to give herself shots, and she had to change her diet. Many people, including her doctors, believed that it would limit what she could do with her life. They were wrong.

Lonely Times

Not long after she was diagnosed with diabetes, Sonia's father died from heart problems caused by his alcoholism. His death made her very sad. It also made life more difficult for the family. Celina worked more than one job to provide for her children. This meant that she wasn't home a lot. Sonia and Junior spent many nights alone at the kitchen table doing their homework.

Sonia faced tough challenges as a child, but they didn't discourage her.

9

"Just Study"

Sonia and Junior attended Blessed Sacrament, a Catholic elementary school. While her children were at school, Celina worked as a telephone operator and later as a nurse. Celina believed in the importance of education. In fact, the Sotomayors were the only family in the Bronxdale Houses to own Encyclopaedia Britannica books. The books were expensive, but Celina wanted her children to learn.

Celina often told Sonia and Junior, "Just study. I don't care what grade you get but just study." Sonia listened. She had an almost perfect attendance record at school and excelled in her studies. She graduated eighth grade as valedictorian.

Sonia graduated eighth grade as valedictorian, meaning she had the best grades in her class.

Sonia returned to Cardinal Spellman High School in 2009 to visit with some current students.

Celina and Sonia had a distant relationship when Sonia was growing up, but now they are very close.

Cardinal Spellman

Sonia attended Cardinal Spellman High School. During Sonia's freshman year, the Sotomayors moved to Co-op City, a large housing development in the Bronx. Despite the transition of moving, Sonia did well in school. She was a member of the student council and on the forensics (debate) team. On weekends and during summers, she worked. Sometimes she mopped the floors in her aunt's store. Other times she washed dishes at a bakery. In 1972 Sonia graduated and was valedictorian once again.

THEN and NOW

Opportunities for Women

When Sonia was growing up, women—especially minority women—did not have the opportunities that they do today. Women had a harder time getting an education than men did. Men were given better jobs than women and made more money. Today things have improved for many women.

Gaining the Tools for Success

Thanks to Sonia's hard work in high school, she received a full scholarship to one of the best colleges in the country: Princeton University in New Jersey. It was not as culturally diverse as the Bronx. As a result, Sonia was very shy at first. She felt as if she was "a visitor landing in an alien country."

Also, her writing skills were not that good. She majored in history and had to write many papers. To improve her writing skills, she got extra help from teachers and read grammar books in her free time. Her confidence grew.

Becoming a Leader

At Princeton University, Sonia became more and more of a presence around campus. She took a job working for the admissions department and became involved in multiple organizations, including the Third World Center group. She became cochair of Acción Puertorriqueña, a group that helped Puerto Rican students. And she served on the student-faculty discipline committee, among other things.

At first Sonia felt out of place at Princeton. But it didn't take her long to become a leader around campus.

Sonia also volunteered. She started an after-school program for local children. She offered her services as an interpreter for Spanish-speaking parents at Trenton Psychiatric Hospital. When she wasn't busy studying, working, or volunteering, Sonia loved to spend time with her friends. They watched Yankees games together and went salsa dancing.

BREAKING BOUNDARIES

LEARNING ENGLISH

Sonia spoke Spanish for most of her childhood. It was not until she was nine that she became fluent in English. Many of her family members, including her father, spoke only Spanish. Sonia worked hard to master both speaking and writing in English.

Making Her Voice Heard

In 1976 Sonia graduated from Princeton summa cum laude. This means that she graduated with the highest honor that a student can receive. Princeton also gave Sonia the M. Taylor Pyne Prize, an award given to a senior for being an outstanding student in and out of the classroom. In her college yearbook, Sonia included a quote from Norman Thomas that hinted toward her future career plans: "I am not a champion of lost causes, but of causes not yet won."

SONIA MARIA SOTOMAYOR

I am not a champion of lost causes, but of causes not yet won.
— Norman Thomas

My Princeton experience has been the people I've met. To them, for their lessons of life, I remain eternally indebted and appreciative. To them and to that extra-special person in my life

Thank You — For all that I am and am not. The sum total of my life here, has been made-up of little parts from all of you.

Sonia's page from her 1976 Princeton yearbook includes a parting message to her classmates.

BREAKING BOUNDARIES

FIGHTING DISCRIMINATION

When Sonia arrived at Princeton, there were no Latino professors, no classes on Latin America, and only 22 Latino students. Sonia met with the school president to discuss changes to reflect more diversity. When no changes were made, she filed a letter of complaint that accused Princeton of discrimination. As a result, Princeton began hiring Latino faculty and recruiting Latino students. Sonia's history professor, Peter Winn, created a class on Puerto Rican history and politics.

THEN and NOW

Diverse Schools

Sonia successfully helped change the population and curriculum of Princeton while she was a student there. A 2009 article in the school's newspaper acknowledged that the university changed some of its practices as a result of Sonia's letter of complaint. Today Princeton and many other colleges across the country have more student and faculty diversity than they did in the 1970s.

Members of Princeton's graduating class celebrate receiving diplomas from one of the nation's most prestigious universities.

Saying Goodbye

Sonia reflected on her time at Princeton:

"Princeton changed us, not just academically, but also in what we learned about life and the world. At the same time, we changed Princeton."

Other Yale Law School graduates include current Supreme Court justices Clarence Thomas (pictured) and Samuel Alito.

Law School

After graduating from Princeton, Sonia knew exactly what she wanted to do next—go to law school and become an attorney (lawyer). She wanted to learn about how the government made and changed laws. She wanted to study those laws. She wanted to understand what lawyers and judges did to pursue fairness and justice for all citizens.

Sonia was accepted to another one of the nation's best universities, Yale Law School, in New Haven, Connecticut. She was given a scholarship. Before she began law school, she married Kevin Noonan on August 14, 1976. They had been dating since high school.

Becoming a Lawyer

It did not take long for Sonia to make her mark at Yale. The student who had once struggled with writing became the editor of the *Yale Law Journal* and the *Yale Studies in World Public Order* (now called *Yale Journal of International Law*). In 1979 Sonia graduated from Yale with a J.D., or Juris Doctor degree. But she was not a lawyer yet. All law students must take a big exam called the bar. In 1980 Sonia passed the New York bar. Sonia from the Bronx was now a lawyer.

Sonia as a Student

People who knew her reflect on what Sonia was like at school:

"She's one of those where, even at a school with great people, I knew that she was going to go on and do amazing things."

—Robert H. Klonoff

"She is a person of passionate commitments and the most important one is her commitment to the rule of law."

—Peter Kougasian

Yale has the most selective law school in the United States.

17

Legal Career Beginnings

Sonia did not hesitate to begin her career. Immediately following her graduation from Yale, she was hired as an assistant district attorney for New York. A district attorney is a public official who represents the government by prosecuting people accused of breaking the law.

Sonia had many responsibilities and worked very long hours. She worked hard to investigate, or gather all of the facts, for her court cases. Sometimes she even visited dangerous neighborhoods to interview witnesses to crimes. Once she had gathered her research, she would write it down. Then she would give presentations to juries, describing the facts she uncovered. All of her hard work paid off. Sonia helped send shoplifters, robbers, and even murderers to jail.

District Attorney Robert Morgenthau, Sonia's boss, was so impressed by Sonia that he gave her a more important job.

An attorney addresses a jury in court.

A Peak Inside a U.S. Courtroom

A person or company that is accused of a crime is given a trial in court. A trial allows both sides of a story to be told. One lawyer, the prosecutor, presents his or her case against the accused to the judge and jury. The prosecutor's job is to prove that the defendant, or person accused, is guilty of the crime. The other lawyer, the defense attorney, represents the defendant and presents a case to prove that the person is not guilty.

Once both sides of the story have been heard, the jury decides who is right based on the laws. The laws depend on where the trial is held. The judge monitors the trial and gives a sentence, or punishment, to the defendant if he or she is proven guilty.

Pavia & Harcourt

After five years at the district attorney's office, Sonia decided that it was time for a change. A change came in both her personal and professional life. In 1983 she divorced her husband, Kevin Noonan. In 1984 she took a job as an associate lawyer at the private law firm of Pavia & Harcourt in Manhattan. It was a completely different kind of job.

At Pavia & Harcourt, Sonia worked to protect her clients from having their products, ideas, and designs copied by other people or companies. This area of law is known as intellectual property. One of her clients was Fendi, a clothing company that also makes expensive purses. People were creating and selling fake versions of Fendi purses. Sonia helped Fendi by stopping other people from selling the fake purses.

BREAKING BOUNDARIES

SOTOMAYOR & ASSOCIATES

Sonia also started her own law practice, Sotomayor & Associates. She ran it from 1983 to 1986 from her Brooklyn apartment. Its main purpose was to help family and friends in their real estate and business planning decisions.

Sonia worked hard as a lawyer for several years in order to fulfill her dream of becoming a judge.

FENDI

Fendi is a designer of luxury clothing and accessories.

Sonia learned very quickly and impressed her employers and coworkers. In fact, the firm was so impressed that it promoted her to partner, which meant that she became part owner of the company, in 1988.

Fact

In 1986 Sonia staged an event known as the "Fendi Crush." Hundreds of fake purses, shoes, and other items were thrown into garbage trucks and smashed. It was a message to stop buying and selling fake products. Partner George M. Pavia said, "It was the pinnacle of our achievement, and Sonia was the principle doer."

Lifelong Philanthropist

Even though Sonia had an incredibly busy schedule, she still found time for philanthropy. She volunteered her services to many causes to help people in need. Aside from being an effective lawyer, Sonia proved to be a champion of public service.

Sonia did a lot of pro bono work, or work for free. From 1980 to 1992, she was on the board of directors for the Puerto Rican Legal Defense Education Fund, which is a national organization that fights for civil rights for the Latino population in the United States.

Sonia loves volunteering, especially for youth organizations.

Fact

Sonia loves to work with children. One of her favorite activities is to run a mock (fake) trial using the story "Goldilocks and the Three Bears" as the subject of the trial. The process helps children understand what lawyers, judges, and other members of the court do.

Helping Others

Sonia also volunteers with other organizations. In 1987 Sonia became the youngest board member of the State of New York Mortgage Agency. The agency works to make housing and insurance more affordable for low-income individuals and families. One children's program that Sonia volunteers for is the Development School for Youth program. It teaches inner-city children about different careers.

Giving Back

Sonia's former classmate at Princeton, Margarita Rosa, said of Sonia:

"I think she has a profound sense of giving back to all communities, but particularly communities that may not have the advantages that others might have."

Sonia prepares to throw the first pitch at a charity softball game.

Judge Sotomayor

Sonia was happy at Pavia & Harcourt, but she never lost hope in her dream to one day become a judge. However, a person can't apply to become a judge; the person must be nominated and then confirmed. Also, there must be an open seat, meaning that a judge must retire or leave the position in order for someone new to fill the spot.

Fact
Federal district judges hear court cases about national law issues, not state law issues. These judges only try cases that occur within their districts. Sonia, for instance, only handled cases that happened in Manhattan, the Bronx, and six counties north of New York City.

Sonia became the first Puerto Rican U.S. federal court judge in 1992.

Sonia said that Senator Moynihan was the "single most important person" behind her nomination.

Sonia had done so well as a lawyer that she had earned a good reputation. Former New York Senator Daniel Patrick Moynihan was impressed with Sonia. He recommended her to President George H.W. Bush as a good choice for federal district judge in the Southern District of New York. President Bush agreed with Moynihan. In November 1991, Bush officially nominated her. Sonia was confirmed as judge for the United States District Court for the Southern District of New York in August 1992. She was now a judge.

BREAKING BOUNDARIES

MAKING HISTORY AGAIN

In achieving her childhood dream of becoming a judge, Sonia made history. At 37 years old, she became the youngest member of the U.S. District Court. She was also the first Hispanic federal judge in New York state and the first Puerto Rican U.S. federal court judge.

Understanding the United States Federal Court System

To understand Sonia's career journey, you need to know about the Judicial Branch of government. There are three branches of government. There's the Legislative Branch, which is made up of Congress (the Senate and the House of Representatives). There's the Executive Branch, which is made up of the president and vice president. And then there's the Judicial Branch, which is made up of the Supreme Court. This is Sonia's branch.

The Judicial Branch

The powers of the Judicial Branch are broken down into three main levels. On the lowest level, there are federal district courts, which is where Sonia was first appointed. There are 94 district courts. On the next level are the 13 circuit courts of appeals. They can overrule, or change, a decision made by any of the district courts.

THEN and NOW

Supreme Court Justices
Established in 1789, the Supreme Court had five associate justices and one chief justice. In 1807 Congress changed the number of associate justices to seven. The number was changed again in 1869, making it eight associate justices and one chief justice. Today, there are still nine members of the Supreme Court.

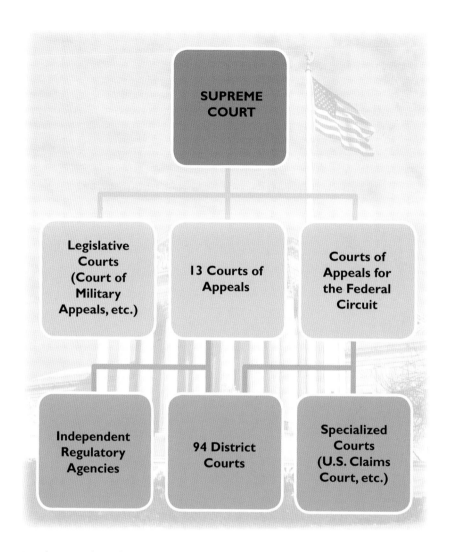

At the top level, holding the most power, is the Supreme Court. The Supreme Court is made up of eight associate justices and one chief justice. They are nominated by the president and approved by the Senate. Once approved, justices serve on the Supreme Court for the rest of their lives unless they choose to retire. The Supreme Court deals with the most important court cases in the United States.

On the Job

Once Sonia put on her black judge's cloak, she wasted no time getting to work. She moved from Brooklyn, where she had been living, back to the Bronx so that she could live within her district. From 1992 to 1998, she presided over more than 450 cases. Her cases dealt with organized crime, illegal drugs, immigration laws, and other things.

As a judge, Sonia was known for being extremely well prepared and strict. She followed in the footsteps of friend and mentor, Judge Miriam Goldman Cedarbaum. Sonia was demanding of both her law clerks and the lawyers who argued their cases in front of her in court. Although she was a tough boss, she had an excellent relationship with her law clerks who helped her research cases. Sonia developed great friendships with many of them and helped guide them in their law careers.

Judge Miriam Goldman Cedarbaum became a federal district judge in 1986. Few women were judges at the time.

Baseball players worked with union chief Donald Fehr (second from left) to end their strike.

The Baseball Strike

One of Sonia's most notable cases came in 1995, when she helped end the longest sports strike in history at the time: the 232-day-long Major League Baseball (MLB) strike. The strike was caused by a disagreement between the team owners and the players. Sonia helped the owners and players come to a compromise, or agreement. It earned her the respect of many baseball fans.

Fact

Sonia performed her first official act as judge the night she was sworn in. She married her mother, Celina, to Omar Lopez, her mother's longtime boyfriend.

Court of Appeals Nomination

On June 25, 1997, Sonia was given very exciting news. President Bill Clinton had nominated her to the Second Circuit of the U.S. Court of Appeals. However, her appointment as court of appeals judge was delayed. Some members of the Senate did not think that Sonia would be able to separate her personal opinions and beliefs from her courtroom case decisions. They questioned her ability to stick to only facts, not feelings.

Waiting to Make History

The Senate held a very long hearing. They asked Sonia many questions. Finally, in March 1998, the Senate approved her nomination. She became a court of appeals judge. Sonia made history once again by being the first Latina judge of this level.

A very happy Sonia poses by her new court of appeals office window in 1998.

Political Opinions

Even though Sonia was nominated to be a court of appeals judge in 1997, her appointment wasn't until 1998. Members of the Senate had differing political opinions of her. Sonia was upset by the accusations. She said,

"It is stereotyping, and stereotyping is perhaps the most insidious of all problems in our society today."

Bill Clinton was president of the United States from 1993 to 2001.

A POWERFUL JUDGE

A court of appeals judge decides appeals (disagreements with verdicts) from the district courts within its circuit. They are the second most powerful judges in the country, under the Supreme Court justices. When Sonia's nomination was approved in 1998, she became the first Latina court of appeals judge.

A Decade of Service

In Sonia's 10 years on the court of appeals, she heard more than 3,000 cases. She wrote 380 papers, or published opinions, about all sorts of issues. She became a member of the Second Circuit Task Force on Gender, Racial, and Ethnic Fairness in the Courts. The task force works to prevent discrimination and bias in the courts.

Sonia worked hard and played hard, and she encouraged her staff to do the same. Many view her judicial approach throughout her time as a court of appeals judge as consistent and fair. Yale professor Stephen Carter said that Sonia "appreciates the complexity of issues" and "reasons to get to the bottom of issues."

As a court of appeals judge, Sonia was known for her attention to detail. She went to great lengths to examine all the facts of each case.

Peter White, Sonia's fiancé, helped her put on her court of appeals robes for the first time. The couple later called off their engagement.

Love of Teaching

When Sonia wasn't busy making important decisions in the courtroom, she taught college classes on law. From 1998 to 2007, she was an adjunct (part-time) professor at New York University School of Law. She began lecturing at Columbia University Law School in New York in 1999 and continues to teach classes there on occasion. Sonia has also lectured at other universities.

Prejudices of Her Own

During a speech in 2001, Sonia made a remark that would later cause her trouble. She said,

> "I would hope that a wise Latina woman with the richness of her experiences would, more often than not, reach a better conclusion than a white male who hasn't lived that life."

This made some people believe that Sonia has prejudices of her own.

History Is Made

In 2009 Justice David Souter decided to retire, so there was an open seat on the Supreme Court. On May 25, 2009, President Barack Obama told Sonia that she was his choice to replace Justice Souter. When Sonia heard the news, she said, "I had my hand over my chest, trying to calm my beating heart, literally."

But Sonia had to be approved by the Senate. She was determined to win over the senators. Just like in 1997 when she was nominated to the court of appeals, Sonia had people who did not want her to be appointed. She visited senators in their offices to talk. She explained that she would be an unbiased justice.

Fact
Sonia broke her ankle in the middle of her Senate visits. However, this didn't stop her from going from office to office on crutches.

Good Judgment

The "wise Latina" comment Sonia made in her speech in 2001 was brought up many times during her confirmation hearing. Several senators did not like it. Sonia said, in her defense,

"I do not believe any ethnic, racial, or gender group has an advantage in sound judgment."

Sonia was asked many questions during the Senate confirmation hearings.

Confirmation Hearings

On July 13, 2009, Sonia appeared before the entire Senate to answer questions. For four days Sonia listened to people testify for and against her nomination. She answered hours of questions about her personal life and decisions she made as a district and court of appeals judge.

Ultimately, on August 6, 2009, the Senate confirmed Sonia as a Supreme Court justice with a vote of 68–31. Sonia from the Bronx had done it.

Sonia and President Obama are two great examples of the American Dream.

Justice Sotomayor

On August 8, 2009, Chief Justice John Roberts swore Sonia in as the 111th associate justice of the Supreme Court. Even Sonia had never dreamed that she'd reach the highest level in the law profession. She expressed her gratitude in front of the nation: "I am an ordinary person who has been blessed with extraordinary opportunities and experiences. It is this nation's faith in a more perfect union that allows a Puerto Rican girl from the Bronx to stand here now."

Many magazines and newspapers marked the confirmation of Sonia Sotomayor as Supreme Court judge.

BREAKING BOUNDARIES

HISPANIC SUPREME COURT JUSTICE

Sonia changed the course of history when she was confirmed. She became the nation's first Hispanic Supreme Court justice. She is the third woman to serve as an associate justice. Also, with her addition, the Supreme Court now holds a record six Roman Catholic justices serving at the same time.

Sandra Day O'Connor was confirmed as a Supreme Court judge in 1981. She served until her retirement in 2006.

THEN and NOW

Female Justices

Sandra Day O'Connor became the first female Supreme Court justice in 1981. She retired in 2006. Ruth Bader Ginsburg followed Justice O'Connor. She was sworn in as the second female Supreme Court justice in 1993. Justice Ginsburg still serves on the court today with Sonia.

Sonia's Journey

Sonia's journey to the Supreme Court is inspiring. Her story suggests that hard work, knowledge, and bravery can help overcome any circumstance, no matter how difficult it may be. Sonia's endless determination is one of the reasons that she holds one of the most important jobs in the country today.

Life in Washington, D.C.

Sonia admitted that her first day of work in the Supreme Court Building in Washington, D.C., was "overwhelmingly terrifying." She was so nervous that her knees knocked. "I thought everybody in the courtroom could hear them knocking," she later said. However, it didn't take Sonia long to settle in. She is currently reviewing many cases on important issues ranging from civil rights to immigration laws. Her decisions will change the country. Some already have.

THEN and NOW

Bronxdale Houses

Sonia grew up in the Bronxdale Houses, an apartment complex. In June 2010, the complex was renamed after her. The Justice Sonia Sotomayor Houses and Justice Sonia Sotomayor Community Center contain 28 buildings and have about 3,500 residents. Today, the neighborhood is safer than it was in the past.

Sonia speaks at the renaming ceremony for the Bronxdale Houses.

38

The nine current Supreme Court justices posed for a photo in March 2012.

More Achievements

Although Sonia has accomplished so much, she continues to set new goals for herself and reach new heights. She has received many awards, including honorary law degrees from several schools. She has given more than 180 speeches to different audiences over the last 30 years. Sonia also continues to volunteer her time and energy to several organizations.

Sonia has not taken a day of her life for granted. She said in a 2013 interview, "I had a life in which I was in a hurry…. And I got in as much as I could do at every stage of my life. I studied very hard. I partied very hard. I love playing very hard. And I did it all to try to pack in as much as I could." Indeed, she has.

Outside the Courtroom

On top of Sonia's hard work in the Supreme Court, she also manages to have fun. She is very close with her family and spends as much time as possible with them. Her brother, Junior, is now a doctor in Syracuse, New York. He is married with three children. Sonia visits them and vacations with them. She also visits her mother, Celina, and her stepfather, Omar, in Florida. Sonia frequently travels to Puerto Rico to see relatives.

Even Justices Have Hobbies

Sonia finds it important to stay healthy and active. She likes to work out and eat nutritious lunches. Two of her favorite foods are tuna fish and cottage cheese.

At night Sonia sometimes attends the theater. She especially loves ballets and operas. She still enjoys salsa dancing. And she is still a loyal fan to her beloved Yankees. She watches them on TV and attends games.

Sonia is a lifelong Yankees fan and enjoys going to games with family and friends.

Sonia has a very special relationship with her family. She is close with her nephews, Conner and Corey.

Working with Children

Sonia's work for youth programs continues to be important to her. In Sonia's 2013 *60 Minutes* interview, she said, "I want one of the hallmarks of my tenure to be that I gave something to kids; that I gave something to our future." Sonia visits classrooms and works with kids to help them learn and realize their dreams. At a 2012 celebration for the Bronx Children's Museum, Sonia told the audience: "Don't ever stop dreaming. Don't ever stop trying. There's courage in trying."

Fact
Sonia was on *Sesame Street* twice in 2012. In her first appearance, she demonstrated how a judge hears a case. The second time, Sonia explained what the word "career" means.

Still Making History

In January 2013 Sonia swore Vice President Joe Biden into his second term in office. This made her the first Hispanic justice to give the oath. Sonia is only the fourth woman to give the oath to a president or vice president.

My Beloved World

Sonia's autobiography, *My Beloved World*, came out on January 15, 2013. It received many excellent reviews. In the book she wrote about her sometimes difficult childhood and credits her stubbornness for certain life successes.

Sonia swore Vice President Joe Biden into his second term in office on January 20, 2012.

Sonia has made her mark on history while giving back to the community.

In *My Beloved World*, Sonia explains that one of the reasons she wrote the book was to help others believe in themselves. She wanted to give her readers hope. "People who live in difficult circumstances need to know that happy endings are possible." Also, she wanted to express the importance of having dreams and setting goals.

What's Next?

This is not the end of Sonia's story. Maybe right now she is busy studying, or even hearing, a case. Or perhaps she is volunteering, teaching, or spending time with family. While she doesn't know what the future holds, Sonia knows that she wants to continue improving herself. "I haven't finished growing yet. I'm young at heart. I'm young in spirit. And I'm still adventurous." What are you going to dream of doing today?

Passion for Law

In a 2013 interview, Sonia claimed that passion is what unites the Supreme Court justices.

"We are all equally passionate about the Constitution, about the country, about what we do."

She went on to say that their love for their job made them friends, not just colleagues.

Glossary

bias attitude that favors one way of feeling or acting over another

civil rights rights of personal liberty (freedom) guaranteed for all American citizens by the 13th and 14th amendments of the Constitution

descent person's line of ancestors

detective person who solves crimes and catches criminals

diagnosed have recognized the signs and symptoms

discrimination treating some people better than others without fair or good reason

diverse differing from one another

editor person who revises and corrects mistakes before publication or print

Hispanic person living in the United States whose ancestors are from Latin America

immigration act of coming to a foreign country to live

insidious something that is harmful and develops slowly

interpreter person who translates orally for people speaking different languages

judge public official who has the authority (power) to decide questions brought before a court

jury group of citizens who are asked to determine whether a person is guilty or not guilty of a crime

justice Supreme Court judge

law clerk person who helps a judge or lawyer

law firm business owned by one or more lawyers to practice law

lawyer person who conducts lawsuits for clients. A lawyer gives clients advice about their legal rights.

mentor person who helps tutor or guide another person

minority part of a population that differs from the majority (larger) population in some characteristics

philanthropy active effort to promote human well being; generous efforts to help others

profession job that requires special knowledge and often an advanced education; career

profound complete; great knowledge or understanding

prosecuting carrying on a legal action against an accused person to prove his or her guilt

scholarship money given to a student to help pay for further education

valedictorian student with the highest rank in a graduating class who gives a speech at graduation ceremonies

verdict decision reached by a jury

witness person who gives evidence before a court of law

Timeline

1954   Sonia Maria Sotomayor is born on June 25th in the Bronx, New York.

1962   Sonia is diagnosed with type 1 diabetes.

1963   Sonia's father, Juan, dies.

1972   Sonia graduates from Cardinal Spellman High School as valedictorian.

1976   Sonia graduates from Princeton University with a degree in history.

1979   Sonia graduates from Yale Law School summa cum laude. She takes a job as assistant district attorney for the state of New York's district attorney office.

1984   Sonia takes a job with a small law firm called Pavia & Harcourt. She later becomes a partner.

1992   Sonia is appointed by President George H.W. Bush to be a U.S. District Court judge for the Southern District of New York.

1998   Sonia is appointed by President Bill Clinton to be a judge on the U.S. Court of Appeals for the Second Circuit.

1999   Sonia begins lecturing at Columbia University Law School in New York City.

2009   President Barack Obama appoints Sonia as associate justice of the U.S. Supreme Court. She is the first Hispanic judge in history and the third female justice.

2013   Sonia publishes her autobiography. She becomes the first Hispanic justice to swear a president or vice president into office.

Find Out More

Books

Bernier-Grand, Carmen T. *Sonia Sotomayor: Supreme Court Justice.* New York: Marshall Cavendish Childrens, 2010.

Gitlin, Marty. *Sonia Sotomayor: Supreme Court Justice.* Edina, Minn.: ABDO, 2011.

McElroy, Lisa Tucker. *Sonia Sotomayor: First Hispanic U.S. Supreme Court Justice.* Minneapolis: Lerner Publications, 2010.

Van Tol, Alex. *Sonia Sotomayor: U.S. Supreme Court Justice.* New York: Crabtree, 2011.

Winter, Jonah. *Sonia Sotomayor: A Judge Grows in the Bronx.* New York: Atheneum Books, 2009.

Websites

bensguide.gpo.gov/
Visit this site to learn how laws are made and other interesting facts.

congressforkids.net/
This site offers a better understanding of the different branches of the U.S. government. Take online quizzes to build your knowledge in a fun way!

kids.usa.gov/
Check out the U.S. government's official website for kids! You can learn about all different subjects—from history to health—as well as watch videos and play games.

usconsulate.org.hk/pas/kids/index.htm
Learn information about the different branches of the U.S. government, famous Americans, and laws.

Further Research

If you enjoyed this book and want to learn more about lawyers and courts, try the following activities.
- Have a mock, or fake, trial with your friends! For examples, check out this website: http://19thcircuitcourt.state.il.us/services/pages/mock_trials.aspx
- Find out where the closest courthouse is where you live. Visit the courthouse and take a tour!

Index